WITH THE BOSTON TEA PARTY

IN UNITED STATES HISTORY

IN
UNITED STATES
★ HISTORY ★

☆ MARY E. HULL ☆

Enslow Publishers, Inc.
40 Industrial Road
Box 398
Berkeley Heights, NJ 07922
USA
http://www.enslow.com

Originally published as *The Boston Tea Party in American History* in 1999.

No part of this book may be reproduced by any means
without the written permission of the publisher.

Library of Congress Cataloging-in-Publication Data

Hull, Mary.
   Witness the Boston Tea Party in United States history / Mary E. Hull.
      pages cm. — (In United States history)
   Includes bibliographical references and index.
   Audience: Grades 4-6.
   ISBN 978-0-7660-6335-8
   1. Boston Tea Party, Boston, Mass., 1773—Juvenile literature. I. Title.
   E215.7.H85 2015
   973.3'115—dc23

                               2014025738

Printed in the United States of America

102014 Bang Printing, Brainerd, Minn.

10 9 8 7 6 5 4 3 2 1

Future Editions:
Paperback ISBN: 978-0-7660-6336-5
EPUB ISBN: 978-0-7660-6337-2
Single-User PDF ISBN: 978-0-7660-6338-9
Multi-User PDF ISBN: 978-0-7660-6339-6

To Our Readers: We have done our best to make sure all Internet addresses in this book were active and appropriate when we went to press. However, the author and the publisher have no control over and assume no liability for the material available on those Internet sites or on other Web sites they may link to. Comments can be sent by e-mail to comments@enslow.com or to the address on the back cover.

🜋 Enslow Publishers, Inc., is committed to printing our books on recycled paper. The paper in every book contains 10% to 30% post-consumer waste (PCW). The cover board on the outside of each book contains 100% PCW. Our goal is to do our part to help young people and the environment too!

Illustration Credits: ©Thinkstock/Steven Wynn/iStock, p. 4; Enslow Publishers, Inc., pp. 63, 83; Library of Congress, p. 1.

Cover Illustration: Library of Congress
Cover Caption: "The Destruction of Tea at Boston Harbor" by Nathaniel Currier.

☆ CONTENTS ☆

After the repeal of the Stamp Act in 1766, colonists in New York City erected a statue of King George. On July 9, 1776 the colonists tore it down after hearing the Declaration of Independence. This engraving depicts the angry mob tearing down the statue.

Chapter 1

TENSION BUILDS IN BOSTON

On December 16, 1773, the colonial port city of Boston was swarming with activity. People had been pouring into the city from the surrounding towns and counties all day. By horse and oxcart, on foot, on horseback, and by ferry they came, responding to the call for a meeting of patriots. Colonists came from as far away as Maine in the hope of reaching a decision about a problem that had long been troubling them. They were upset over the passage of the Tea Act of 1773.

The Tea Act was a British law that required the colonies to pay a tax on tea imported from England. Rather than pay the tax, many colonists wanted to boycott tea and stop all shipments from England. However, the first ships bearing tea subject to the Tea Act had already arrived in Boston Harbor, and under British law the tax had to be paid on the cargoes of all vessels entering the harbor. That day, December 16, was the final day before the tax was due. If the citizens of Boston did not take immediate action against the newly arrived tea ships, the tax on the cargoes would be paid by the owners of the merchandise. Then the tea would be unloaded, and every person who purchased tea would, in turn, be paying the hated tea tax. By submitting to the tax, American colonists would be admitting the right of the British Parliament (legislature) to tax them, and they would be going along with a law they detested. The ships waiting to be unloaded in Boston Harbor had created a crisis.

Opposing the Tax on Tea

Since the Townshend Acts of 1767, which placed a tax on tea and other household items, American colonists had been opposed to the taxing of tea. Although tea was a popular drink, many colonists preferred to go without it rather than submit to what they believed was an unfair tax. Instead of buying imported tea, the colonists brewed homemade herbal substitutes. The boycotting of tea imported from England became a symbol of defiance that united protesters in all the American colonies.

The colonists opposed the Townshend Acts and the Tea Act because the revenues they raised were to pay the salaries of Great Britain's colonial administrators. Previously, these officials had been dependent on the colonial legislatures for their salaries. The colonists were upset about the change. They wanted to be able to control the officials' salaries. That way, the officials would be accountable to them instead of to England. Furthermore, under the Tea Act, tea was to be sold only by authorized merchants. Those merchants had been selected by the East India Company, a British trading enterprise and the only one allowed to import tea into America. This provision caused many colonists to fear that the Tea Act might be the first step in giving the East India Company a monopoly on colonial trade, which would hurt many colonial businessmen by taking away their jobs.

The Years of Neglect

The Tea Act of 1773 was the latest in a series of controversial acts that had annoyed the colonists over the course of a decade. Much of the friction between England and the American colonies stemmed from the fact that for many decades, England had basically ignored the colonies. The British government had also failed to enforce tax collection. This period was known as the years of salutary, or beneficial, neglect. During this time, colonists had grown accustomed to being left alone. They enjoyed the freedom the neglect gave them. They were able to ignore many laws, which were seldom enforced by Crown officials, who were often corrupt. The colonists also made money by smuggling cheaper, non-British goods into colonial harbors. Under British law, the colonists were only supposed to import British East India Company tea. But a long-standing smuggling ring in the colonies brought Dutch tea into America. The smuggled tea was much cheaper, and came from the same Chinese ports as British tea. Beginning in

1763, however, a British crackdown on smuggling made it harder for the colonists to import Dutch tea.

By 1763, after England had defeated France in the Seven Years' War, the years of salutary neglect were over. Strapped for cash and saddled with a massive war debt, England began to try to raise money from its colonies. Parliament subjected the colonies to several new tax measures, including the Sugar Act, the Stamp Act, and the Townshend duties. The colonists resented these taxes and feared that the British East India Company would be given a complete monopoly on all colonial trade, raising prices on imported goods to unfair levels.

Throughout the colonies, committees of concerned citizens, calling themselves patriots, organized to oppose these British policies. The patriots, considered rabble-rousers by British authorities, held mass meetings. They organized protests and demonstrations to express their distaste for British policies. In the colony of Massachusetts, patriots formed clubs such as the Loyal Nine, composed of key leaders, and the Boston Committee of Correspondence, which wrote to patriot groups in the other colonies, keeping them informed of events in Boston. Many people who would later become famous patriots, such as Samuel Adams, Joseph Warren, and Paul Revere, were involved in these groups. The committees of correspondence in all the colonies shared an interest in achieving greater freedom for the colonists.

The Arrival of the *Dartmouth*

The arrival of the *Dartmouth*, the first tea ship subject to the Tea Act, on November 28, 1773, touched off a series of town meetings. A committee of patriots asked the merchants to whom the tea shipment had been sent to resign their posts as the official merchants of East India Company tea. The merchants refused and insisted that the ship's cargo be unloaded. The patriots, however, would not import any British tea. They hoped that an order from a twenty-three-year-old Quaker man named Francis Rotch, one of the ship's owners, could turn the ship around and send it back to England before any taxes would have to be paid. Under the terms of the Townshend Act, however, any ship entering Boston Harbor was subject to an import duty, a tax on all its contents. By the time the patriots learned of the ship's arrival, it had already entered the harbor.

Still hoping to force the ship to return to England, the committee of correspondence asked Rotch not to report the arrival of his ship to customs until the last possible moment. The committee knew that once its arrival was reported, the ship surely would not be allowed to leave until the duty was paid.

Rotch was pressured by the patriots. At first, he went along with them, agreeing not to unload his ship and to send it back to England. Later, on the advice of his lawyers and his father, Rotch claimed that returning the cargo would ruin him financially.

Sounding the Alarm

To enlist help in opposing the unloading of the tea ships, patriots in Boston sent express riders into the countryside. The riders' job was to inform people of what was going on in Boston. The riders carried letters telling of the tea's arrival and of a meeting to be held the next morning at Faneuil Hall. Built in Boston in 1742, Faneuil Hall was a waterfront meetinghouse and marketplace. The letters asked every citizen to help the patriots in their fight against British tyranny. The Loyal Nine hung posters announcing the meeting:

> Friends! Brethren! Countrymen! That worst of plagues, the detested tea, shipped for this port by the East India Company, is now arrived in this harbor; the hour of destruction or manly opposition to the machinations [schemes] of tyranny stares you in the face; every friend to his country, to himself, and posterity [history] is now called upon to meet at Faneuil Hall, at nine o'clock this day, (at which time the bells will ring), to make a united and successful resistance to this last, worst and most destructive measure of administration.
>
> —Boston, November 29, 1773[1]

The commotion caused by the arrival of the *Dartmouth* in Boston linked patriots from both the country and the city in common concern and protest to the unfair British laws. As one colonist wrote in a letter to his friend,

> Upon the arrival of the tea, an assembly of the people was called—it proved as large as any ever known here. . . . Great numbers from the neighboring towns united in it,

and, indeed, the people in the country have all along been equally zealous with their brethren in Boston, in this common cause; and there is now established a correspondence and union between them, never known before.[2]

At nine o'clock the next morning, around five thousand concerned colonists, about a third of Boston's total population, crowded into Faneuil Hall. The leading patriots of Boston spoke about the fate of the tea ship. The meeting, moderated by John Hancock, a wealthy merchant and outspoken patriot, was orderly. The patriots referred to those assembled as "the body."[3]

It was soon discovered that the crowd was too large to fit inside Faneuil Hall, and the meeting was moved to a larger structure, the Old South Meeting House. There, the body approved motions made by Samuel Adams to prevent the unloading of the tea, to refuse to pay any duty on the cargo, and to return it to England.

Dr. Thomas Young, a member of the Sons of Liberty, a patriot organization, spoke up. Foreshadowing the events to come, he suggested that the only way to get rid of the tea might be to dump it overboard. The body, respectful of private property, disagreed. They wanted the tea to remain untouched so that it might be returned to the British East India Company.

Rotch then appealed to the crowd. He pleaded with them, saying that if he sent his ship back without permission from customs, it would be seized and his career would be ruined. The members of the meeting advised him to apply to customs for permission to leave the harbor and return his cargo to England.

A motion was also made to designate six experienced horseback riders as messengers. These riders were to be ready to give an alarm to the country towns in order to keep people informed of events in Boston.

In a final motion before adjourning, the body voted to place an armed guard made up of twenty-five colonists aboard the *Dartmouth*. These guards were to prevent any surprise attempt, by merchants or by anyone else, to bring the tea on land. A new group of twenty-five men would be put on guard each evening until the vessel left the harbor.

Guarding the *Dartmouth*

At nine o'clock that same evening, the first group of guards, all volunteers, boarded the *Dartmouth*. The *Dartmouth* was anchored by Fort William, which was known as the Castle because it was fortified with British cannons. A sign-up sheet for guard duty was hung at the printing office of Edes & Gill, whose owners frequently printed posters for the patriot cause. The *Dartmouth* guards over the next few weeks included patriots such as John Hancock and Henry Knox, who would later become George Washington's artillery commander in the American Revolution.

To further protect the tea on the ship, the patriots hung posters around town. They warned that anyone caught unloading the vessels would be dealt with by the mob. The posters were signed, "The People."

Drafting a Resolution

Another mass meeting was held at the Old South Meeting House on November 30 at 9:00 A.M. There, the assembled crowd learned that Rotch had failed to gain clearance for his ship from customs and that the merchants still refused to return the tea. Rotch was reluctant to send the tea ship back to England because he had been unable to get a pass for it. Without clearance, the ship might be sunk by the British or captured and seized under the revenue laws. The Crown would then own the ship and all its contents.

Following this news from Rotch, a proclamation from Governor Thomas Hutchinson of Massachusetts was read to the crowd. Hutchinson, an American who worked as an officer of the British government, was an unpopular figure. His proclamation ordered everyone present to disperse, leave, and not to engage in any more such meetings. The crowd hissed when the proclamation was read.

The moderator of the meeting asked the people present if they wanted to obey the governor's order. The body voted to ignore Hutchinson's proclamation, and the meeting continued. The people at the meeting then wrote their own resolution, detailing their intention to prevent the unloading of the tea. It also expressed their willingness to defend the resolution at the risk of their own lives and property. Copies of this resolution were sent to New York and Philadelphia, where the news of Boston's bravery was received with cheers and the ringing of bells.

The Loyalists Become Alarmed

The patriots' resistance grew. Customs officers and tea merchants began to worry that they would become the targets of mob violence if they did not comply with the patriots' demands. In November a store owned by Richard Clarke, a tea agent for the British East India Company, had been damaged by a mob demanding that Clarke resign his post. Other merchants had been threatened with tarring and feathering, a peculiar form of torture. Hot tar would be poured over the victim's body, which would then be covered with feathers plucked from barnyard fowl. The victim would be forced to parade through town to his humiliation. When the tar cooled, it could not be removed without pulling the skin off with it, causing pain, scarring, and sometimes death.

Rather than let the patriots make good on their threats, Governor Hutchinson encouraged the customs officers and tea consignees (merchants) to take refuge at Fort William. The governor, who had initially dismissed the mass meetings as nothing but "rabble" run by only the lower classes, was beginning to worry.[4] Alarmed by the growing anger of the townspeople, he wrote to Lord William Dartmouth, England's secretary of state for

America: "I scarcely think they will prosecute these mad resolves; yet it is possible, and if it becomes probable I shall be under necessity of withdrawing to the Castle also, in order to defeat them as far as shall be in my power."[5]

The patriots feared that Governor Hutchinson might react by sending soldiers to overpower the *Dartmouth*'s guards and unload the tea. To prevent this from happening, they asked Rotch to move the ship to Griffin's Wharf, the downtown Boston waterfront. Rotch readily agreed to the move, for in addition to tea, he had a cargo of whale oil on board that he was anxious to unload and sell. With the ship anchored downtown, the patriots felt confident that they could call on the power of the mob, if necessary, to stop the royal forces if they tried to unload the tea.

By December 7, two more tea ships had arrived in Boston Harbor. One, the *Eleanor*, was anchored beside the *Dartmouth* at Griffin's Wharf. The other ship, the *Beaver*, was quarantined at Raninsford's Island in Boston Harbor because of an outbreak of smallpox on board. Even though it was quarantined, the patriots kept an eye on the *Beaver*, insisting that quarantine officials not allow any tea chests to be unloaded. After smoke was forced through the ship (the customary method of cleaning infected ships), the *Beaver* was also moved to Griffin's Wharf. The fourth and final tea ship slated for

Boston, the *William*, never arrived. It ran aground and was wrecked on the shore near Cape Cod, Massachusetts.

On December 8, Governor Hutchinson gave the order that no ship was to leave Boston Harbor without a pass. The royal flagship, the chief ship of British Navy Admiral John Montagu, was strategically stationed to block the outgoing channels.

A United Resistance

Meanwhile, in Philadelphia and New York, no tea ships subject to the new tax had arrived since the Tea Act had been passed. Colonists there had managed to force the colonial tea merchants for the British East India Company to resign. People in Massachusetts knew this because the committees of correspondence in the northern colonies helped keep one another informed about the tea boycott.

Communication with Charleston, South Carolina, however, was so slow that Boston did not know that the *London*, a ship carrying tea from England, had arrived there on December 2. In Charleston, patriots had held a mass meeting, declaring their intention to refuse to import or buy any tea. The *London*'s cargo remained aboard for twenty days and was later stored in the marketplace exchange building.

On Monday, December 13, the *Boston Gazette* printed news from Philadelphia: "Our tea consignees have all resigned, and you need not fear: the tea will not be landed here nor at New York. All that we fear is, that you will shrink at Boston . . . May God give you virtue enough to save the liberties of your country!"[6]

Boston was not about to give up the fight. On the very day that the news from Philadelphia arrived, the Boston Committee of Correspondence had called a meeting of representatives from the five neighboring towns. The meeting began at 9:00 A.M. and ran well into the evening. Though the committee's minutes state that no important business was transacted that day, the patriots there were probably planning the Boston Tea Party.

Another mass meeting was scheduled for the next day, Tuesday, December 14. Once again, Francis Rotch was called before the body. Samuel Adams scolded him for failing to carry out the patriots' demands. Once again, Adams asked Rotch to request a clearance from customs. The seizure deadline, by which time the tax must be paid or else the ship's cargo would be seized, was just two days away. Although neither Rotch nor the patriots expected that he would be granted a pass, Adams wanted to make it clear that the patriots had tried to do everything in their power to send the ship back to England.

Showdown

On December 16, 1773, concerned colonists streamed into Boston from the countryside. There was one day left before the *Dartmouth*'s cargo was to be confiscated by customs officials for failure to pay the import duty. Customs officers would then seize the cargo, bring it on land, and distribute it to the Crown-appointed merchants.

Around 10:00 A.M., a crowd, reportedly seven thousand strong, gathered at the Old South Meeting House, spilling out and surrounding it. Samuel P. Savage, from the town of Weston, Massachusetts, presided over the meeting. Rotch was again called before the body. This time he was ordered to dispatch his vessel, with or without permission. Rotch had been unable to obtain clearance from customs. He explained once again that to try to leave without permission would result in the seizure of his ship and a loss to his livelihood. He was then ordered to go directly to Governor Hutchinson to plead for a pass authorizing his ship to leave the harbor. If he could get a pass and special permission from the governor, he might be allowed to leave Boston Harbor and take his ship back to England as the colonists hoped. Since Governor Hutchinson was staying at his home in Milton, about seven miles away, the meeting adjourned to allow Rotch time to travel there and back.

Although the meeting reconvened at 3:00 P.M., Rotch did not appear. Tension mounted. The patriots were running out of time. The body grew impatient and demanded that action be taken. It was almost dark and the church was lit with candles when Rotch finally reappeared. Governor Hutchinson had refused to grant Rotch's ship a pass to leave the harbor. John Rowe, a prominent citizen of Boston, then spoke up, wondering aloud, "Who knows how tea will mingle with salt water?"[7]

Immediately, cries of "A mob! A mob!" rang through the assembled crowd.[8] Thomas Young, one of the Sons of Liberty, jumped to Rotch's defense. He announced that he expected Rotch's property and person would not be harmed by any mob, explaining that Rotch had cooperated as much as he could. Rotch could not order his ship to return with the tea aboard because if he did, he would lose his ship and a great deal of money. Young then asked Rotch whether he intended to unload the tea in Boston. Rotch replied that to protect himself, he would, if asked by royal authorities, unload the tea.

At this admission, Samuel Adams rose and announced that every tactic within the patriots' power had been tried. They could do nothing more to try to protect their rights. This appeared to be a signal, for immediately, as if on cue, a shout rose from the back of the crowd: "Boston Harbor a tea-pot tonight! Hurrah for Griffins Wharf! The Mohawks are come! Every man to his tent!"[9]

A war whoop was unleashed from the gallery. It was picked up by a group of colonists at the doorway who were disguised as Mohawk Indians. The noise was deafening as the meeting's participants streamed into the streets. "You'd of thought that the inhabitants of the infernal regions had broke loose," said John Andrews, a merchant who lived three blocks away.[10] The colonists were about to take matters into their own hands.

WE WANT TO BE LEFT ALONE

Great Britain had a simple reason for finally enforcing taxation in the colonies. In 1763, following its victory over France in the Seven Years' War (called the French and Indian War in the colonies), Great Britain had an enormous war debt. The interest alone on this war debt amounted to more than 5 million pounds a year, almost as much as the total amount Great Britain would have spent in previous years. (A pound is the British unit of currency, like the American dollar.) The British prime minister decided that since people living in Great Britain were already heavily taxed, the American colonists should help pay off this debt. Compared with their counterparts in England, American subjects were only lightly taxed.

The colonists, however, did not believe the British Parliament had the right to tax them, since the colonists had not elected any of the officials. In America, people believed that only those officials directly elected by the population were capable of representing their interests. The British held a different idea of representation. These different beliefs about representation caused friction between the colonies and England.

Actual versus Virtual Representation

The American colonists had no directly elected representatives in Parliament. Instead, their legislative representatives were elected by the British. The colonists did not appreciate being taxed by people whom they had not elected. They claimed that there should be "no taxation without representation." King George III; Prime Minister George Grenville, the king's most important advisor; and the members of Parliament considered themselves the representatives of all British subjects, whether living in England or abroad. However, the colonists felt that people who did not live in the colonies could not represent their interests. The colonists had grown accustomed to being left alone and to electing their own legislators for their local assemblies.

The British government saw things very differently. It believed in the theory of virtual representation, by which Parliament collectively represented the entire population of Great Britain, including the colonies. The colonists, though, believed in actual representation, whereby specific legislators stood for the interests of specific groups. These two different beliefs about representation became the source of many disagreements.

More disagreement arose from England's economic policy. When England taxed the Americans in order to raise money, the colonists protested.

Mercantilism

The major reason Great Britain established colonies in the first place was for trade. Under an economic policy known as mercantilism, Great Britain planned to make money through its colonies. This was accomplished by importing raw materials from the colonies, converting them to different products, then exporting the manufactured goods back to the colonies. All trade was handled by the British East India Company, a joint-stock corporation formed in the seventeenth century. This type of corporation pooled the resources of many investors (who then held the stock jointly) in order to finance expensive trading expeditions. In India, where the company established a trading station, it was able to gain territorial power. The East India Company laid the basis for the British empire in India. The company sold goods such as tea and fabric, which came from China and India, to all the British colonies.

To help raise money from its colonies, in the seventeenth century, Great Britain passed laws known as the Navigation Acts. These laws allowed only British and colonial ships to trade with the colonies, making it impossible for other countries to benefit from colonial trade. The Navigation Acts said that all American products, including timber, furs, wool, sugar, tobacco, and indigo (a plant used to make blue dye), could be sold only to Great Britain. Foreign goods had to pass through England first, even if they came from countries close to America. This was because foreign goods were subject to import duties before being sold in America.

Trade rules like these were designed to benefit England more than the colonies. For years the trade rules went unchallenged only because they were so easy for the colonists to evade. During the years of salutary neglect, the colonists smuggled goods freely and avoided tax payments with the help of corrupt Crown officials.

In 1763 King George III chose George Grenville as his prime minister. Grenville began looking for ways to pay off England's war debt and to raise money from the colonies. When England decided to start enforcing its revenue laws seriously, the colonists and the British government came into conflict.

Grievances of the Colonists

Among the most detested of all colonial laws were the Writs of Assistance—general search warrants that gave customs officials the authority to search any home or warehouse for smuggled goods. The colonists hated the Writs of Assistance because they were an invasion of privacy and because they cut into colonial smuggling. In 1760, lawyer James Otis quit his position as an official in the British government to argue against the Writs of Assistance, which he called "instruments of slavery . . .

and villainy."[1] He wrote a pamphlet called *The Rights of the British Colonies Asserted and Proved*, which became very popular in the colonies. Despite his arguments that the writs violated the freedom of the colonists, the laws remained in place.

The Sugar and Currency Acts of 1764 also angered the colonists. The Sugar Act was the first law whose sole purpose was to raise money for Great Britain. It taxed the trade on sugar and changed customs regulations in order to stop the smuggling of molasses. Molasses was one of the most popular items of trade in the colonies and was often smuggled. The Currency Act outlawed the paper money issued by the colonies, forcing the colonists to rely solely on hard currency such as silver or gold.

Faced with increased customs duties and a shortage of currency, Americans protested the acts. Eight colonial legislatures petitioned Parliament, claiming that the Sugar Act hurt their commerce and that they had not agreed to its passage. But their complaints were ignored, and Prime Minister Grenville instituted yet another revenue act.

The Stamp Act

With the Stamp Act of 1765, Grenville proposed a tax on printed materials in the colonies. Items such as newspapers, legal deeds, pamphlets, and playing cards would have a stamp put on them to prove that the tax had been paid. People living in England had been subject to this tax for many years, but this was the first time a direct, internal tax had been imposed on goods moving within the colonies.

The colonists immediately rejected the tax, insisting that Parliament had no authority to tax them. When news of the Stamp Act first reached the colonies, only the Virginia legislature was in session. Patrick Henry led the fight to pass the Virginia Stamp Act Resolves, seven measures that protested the Stamp Act so strongly that some people called them treasonous. The first four resolves were accepted and passed. They stressed that the colonists could not be taxed without being represented fairly, and that only colonial legislatures had the right to tax the colonies. Furthermore, the colonists did not have to obey laws passed by Parliament.

Around the colonies, the Stamp Act was resisted. Angry colonists protested by organizing boycotts of British goods.

The Massachusetts legislature also drafted a set of resolves, written by Samuel Adams, that protested the Stamp Act. They were written in such a radical tone that Thomas Hutchinson, then the lieutenant governor of Massachusetts, feared they were practically a declaration of independence from England. Then James Otis, who had become a leader in the Massachusetts House of Representatives, had an idea. He proposed a Stamp Act Congress. All the colonial legislatures could meet to discuss the Stamp Act and what could be done to protest it.

The Massachusetts House of Representatives sent letters to all the other colonial legislatures, inviting them to the Stamp Act Congress. They recommended meeting in the central location of New York City. Nine colonies sent delegations to New York. The Stamp Act Congress met for eighteen days, discussing the situation and writing petitions to King George III and to Parliament's House of Lords and House of Commons.

Lieutenant Governor Hutchinson remarked that the Stamp Act Congress had no authority to convene, and for this reason its petitions were ignored in Great Britain. Still, the Stamp Act Congress was a triumph for the colonies. It marked the first time that they had united in common concern and was an important step toward collective opposition to England.

Stamp Act Riots

In Boston, rioting broke out when ordinary citizens protested the Stamp Act. On August 14, 1765, a straw-stuffed figure made to resemble Andrew Oliver, the Crown-appointed distributor of stamps, was hung from the branches of the Liberty Tree in downtown Boston.

The Liberty Tree was an elm tree used by Boston patriots as a site for demonstrations. It stood at the intersection of what are now Essex and Washington streets. The tree was also right outside the offices of the Boston distillery of Chase and Speakman. Boston patriots frequently held meetings in the upstairs office of Chase and Speakman, and it was these patriots who christened the elm the Liberty Tree.

Hundreds of spectators came to gawk at the figure hanging on the Liberty Tree. That evening, a mob gathered in town. The mob was made up of gangs from the North and South ends of Boston.

The North End and the South End gangs were formed around the annual November 5 celebration of Pope's Day in Boston. Pope's Day, or Guy Fawkes Day, as it is also called, celebrated the anniversary of the exposure of the Gunpowder Plot in England. In 1605, Catholic opponents of the Protestant king, James I, were angry over the king's refusal to tolerate Catholicism. With the help of explosives expert Guy Fawkes, they attempted to blow up the king and Parliament with gunpowder, although they were discovered and executed before they could carry out their plot. Each year on November 5, Protestant men and boys in Boston celebrated Pope's Day by building a "pope's cart," a wagon with a cross or Catholic icon affixed to it. Following the cart and the gang leader, they would enter into rowdy brawls with men in other neighborhoods. The brawlers would fight their neighbors with clubs and sticks. The general spirit of rivalry existed between the gangs year-round.

Samuel Adams tried to make use of the power of these neighborhood gangs. He enlisted their support in the patriot cause. The North End and the South End gangs united to protest the Stamp Act.

Ebenezer Mackintosh, a shoemaker and a veteran of the French and Indian War, had been the South End gang leader. He became known as the Captain of the Liberty Tree when the North End and the South End gangs united to protest the Stamp Act. He helped lead the mob that formed around the Liberty Tree on the night of August 14, 1765. They cheered at the effigy, or stuffed figure, of Andrew Oliver that hung there. Then they burned a nearby building that had been designated as the stamp distribution center. Next, the mob turned on Andrew Oliver's home. They axed open the doors to his house and broke his windows. Terrified, Oliver shouted at the mob from his balcony. He said he would resign from his position if the crowd would back off. Oliver's home was spared.

On the following night, however, another mob gathered outside the homes of other unpopular Tories. (Tories were people who were sympathetic to the British government.) The mob, again composed of local gang members eager to help the patriot cause, began targeting the homes of customs officials who worked to enforce the trade laws. Breaking windows and ransacking cellars, the mob worked its way through selected Tory homes in Boston that night. They attacked the home of William Story, the keeper of records in the new Admiralty Court, which had been set up to enforce the trade laws. Story's windows were broken and some men entered his house, tossing his books and papers into the street. Next, the mob attacked the home of Benjamin Hallowell, a chief customs officer. Hallowell had just finished building his home. The mob broke down the front door and ruined the first floor of his house. They even ransacked his wine cellar, taking liquor for themselves to drink. The mob grew larger, more destructive, and more out of control as it moved from home to home throughout the night.

The Mob Destroys Hutchinson's Home

With Ebenezer Mackintosh in the lead, the angry mob came to the home of Lieutenant Governor Thomas Hutchinson in the North End. Hutchinson's house was one of the finest and most expensively furnished in all of Boston. Hutchinson had just sat down to supper with his five children when word came that a mob was approaching. Instructing his children to hide at the neighbors' house, Hutchinson decided to stay and face the crowd. His oldest daughter, Sally, however, declared that she would not leave without her father. He finally agreed to hide in his sister's nearby house. It is possible that Sally saved her father's life that day.

What happened next was one of the most violent, destructive acts ever witnessed in the city of Boston. The mob broke down the door to Hutchinson's house, entered, and began sacking the home. They stole all of his silver, money, family pictures, and belongings. The mob destroyed the home, breaking furniture and tearing down walls. The books in Hutchinson's library, probably the largest in Boston, were destroyed.

Hutchinson remarked that by the next morning, "one of the best finished houses in the Province had nothing remaining but the bare walls and floors."[2] According to him, the mob was

> not content with tearing off all the wainscot and hangings and splitting the doors to pieces; they beat down the partition walls, and although that alone cost them near[ly] two hours, they cut down the cupola, and they began to take the slate and boards from the roof, and were prevented only by the approaching daylight from a total demolition of the building.[3]

Lieutenant Governor Hutchinson, distraught by the loss of his home and possessions, was comforted somewhat by reports that the organizers of the mob never intended the situation to become so violent or destructive.[4] Indeed, people throughout the city expressed their disgust with the mob for its careless destruction of private property. "Captain" Mackintosh was arrested for his role in the incident, but he was released after unidentified men of means spoke to the sheriff. Several other rioters were also arrested. They were later set free by some prominent men of Boston who entered the jailhouse at night and forced the jailer to release the men.

Stamp Act riots occurred not just in Boston but all around the colonies. A mob in Charleston, South Carolina, also took to the streets. Shouting "Liberty!" they demanded that the city's stamp distributor resign. In Philadelphia, a mob tried to attack Benjamin Franklin's house. Franklin, who worked as a colonial representative in London, had helped one of his friends get a job as a stamp distributor. As a result, the mob thought Franklin was partly responsible for the Stamp Act. Franklin's friends in Philadelphia were able to stop the mob, help protect Franklin's family, and save his house.

Forming a Resistance

The patriot group known as the Sons of Liberty grew out of the resistance to the Stamp Act. The group was a loosely organized network of patriots in all the major colonial cities who were committed to greater freedom for the colonies. The Sons of Liberty were the driving force behind public demonstrations against the British government. They were able to stir up the emotions of ordinary people and involve them in political action. By holding mass meetings, the Sons of Liberty educated ordinary people about the effects of the Stamp Act. They explained how it violated their right to representation, and they stirred up public support for the resistance movement. To protest the Stamp Act, they encouraged people to stop buying British goods. This was known as nonimportation. By refusing to import

British goods, colonists intended to hurt the English economy.

In Boston, the Sons of Liberty consisted of approximately three hundred members drawn from all walks of life—merchants, doctors, blacksmiths, printers, carpenters, and silversmiths, for example. The men belonged to the Whig political party, which opposed the ruling, or Tory, party. Whigs favored greater independence for the colonies and sought to limit royal authority. Tories, by contrast, were loyal to the British government and sought to uphold the power of the Crown.

Most men who joined the Sons of Liberty were affiliated with other clubs, groups, and organizations in the city. Many Sons of Liberty were members of the Ancient and Honorable Artillery Company (a local militia) or the Freemasons (a fraternal brotherhood). Other Sons of Liberty belonged to the Long Room Club, a group of intellectuals that included Samuel Adams; William Molineux, a businessman, smuggler, and prominent patriot; and Joseph Warren, a physician and politically active patriot. Many were members of neighborhood groups like the North End and the South End gangs, which had united to protest the Stamp Act. A group called the Loyal Nine emerged to lead the Sons of Liberty. Despite their ability to rally the people, the Sons of Liberty remained shrouded in secrecy and never took credit for their work. They were happy to remain unnoticed so that the Tories would not know who they were.

Another group affiliated with the Sons of Liberty was the North End Caucus. Organized by Joseph Warren, its sixty-one original members were mostly *mechanics*—the colonial term for artisans and skilled laborers. Often meeting at the Green Dragon Tavern, the North End Caucus formed committees of public service and defense. Its meetings were held in secret, and every member swore not to discuss proceedings with anyone except their leaders. According to member Paul Revere,

> We were so careful that our meetings should be kept secret, that every time we met, every person swore upon the Bible not to discuss any of our transactions, but to [John] Hancock, [Joseph] Warren, or [Dr. Benjamin] Church [another patriot leader] and one or two more leaders.[5]

Private passwords were used by club members to protect themselves from Tory spies.

Despite these precautions, one prominent patriot, Dr. Benjamin Church, later became a Tory spy. In exchange for money, he gave the Tories information about many of the patriots' revolutionary plans. When this was discovered, Church was court-martialed and deported from the country.

Patriot groups like the Sons of Liberty helped organize the Stamp Act protests. Eventually, fear of mob action and public condemnation caused many colonial officials to resign. By November 1, 1765—the date the Stamp Act was supposed to take effect—every colonial stamp distributor had resigned.

Nonimportation was also adversely affecting British businessmen. Many colonial merchants had stopped importing goods from England in order to protest the Stamp Act. Some continued to smuggle goods into the colonies. American merchant John Hancock, who maintained a large fleet of merchant ships, told his agents in London:

> In case the Stamp Act is not repealed my orders are that you will not . . . ship one article. I have wrote . . . this in consideration of the united resolves of not only the principal merchants of this town, but of those of the other trading towns of this province, and which I am determined to abide by.[6]

London merchants whose businesses had been hurt by colonial nonimportation urged Parliament to repeal the Stamp Act. Meanwhile, changes were taking place in the British government. Lord Grenville had been replaced as prime minister by Lord Charles Rockingham. Rockingham thought the Stamp Act was too controversial, and he wanted it repealed.

In March 1766, Parliament repealed the Stamp Act. But the crisis was not yet over. The Stamp Act was replaced with a new measure, the Declaratory Act of 1766, which stated that Great Britain had the right to tax the American colonies and pass legislation for them.

Despite the passage of the Declaratory Act, Bostonians rejoiced at the repeal of the Stamp Act. As soon as the news arrived from England on one of John Hancock's ships, the colonists held a day of celebration. They lit fireworks, fired cannons, and hung lanterns on the Liberty Tree. Bands played and people celebrated throughout the city. John Hancock even supplied the crowd with barrels of Madeira wine, which were rolled onto Boston Common, the city's public park and meeting grounds.

The colonists felt loyal to Great Britain once again. In New York City, colonists were so overjoyed by the repeal of the Stamp Act that they erected a statue of King George III. Few colonists could foresee that their problems with the mother country were far from over.

3 Chapter

THE COLONISTS RESIST

The protests against the Stamp Act showed that American colonists felt alienated from the mother country. In the years following 1763, the colonies had been growing apart from the British monarchy. During this time, King George III replaced his prime ministers several times. These frequent changes in the government created a sense of instability. In 1765, George III replaced Lord Grenville with Lord Rockingham, who was then replaced by William Pitt in 1767. Since Pitt's health was poor, the driving force behind his ministry became Charles Townshend, the chancellor of the exchequer, who was determined to squeeze as much money as possible from the colonies. Pitt was, in turn, replaced by Lord Frederick North in 1770. Each minister had different plans for making money off the colonies. Not surprisingly, the colonists protested each new tax measure. The most controversial plan of all was that of Charles Townshend.

Just one year after the repeal of the Stamp Act, Townshend proposed new taxes, which Parliament passed as the Townshend duties, part of the Townshend Acts, in 1767. The Townshend duties taxed the trade of paper, painters' lead, glass, and tea, all of which were imported frequently by the American colonies. Under the new law, a tax would have to be paid at the port of entry on all these items. Because the cost of importing these items would increase, merchants would then have to make up for the loss by increasing their prices to consumers.

The Townshend Acts

The Townshend duties were different from all previous taxes levied on the colonists. First, they taxed many items, including those imported from England, not just those from foreign countries. Second, they were designed to raise funds for a specific cause. The revenue raised by the Townshend duties would pay the salaries of royal officials in the colonies. This decision angered the colonists, who had been paying these salaries themselves. The colonists had wielded power because they could threaten to withhold officials' salaries. If a royal commissioner, for example, did not behave as the colonists wanted him to, they could simply refuse to pay him. The Townshend Acts took away this power.

Colonists also hated the Townshend Acts because they made it easier for royal officials to collect taxes. The acts created a new customs system with admiralty courts to enforce the law in the port cities of Boston, Philadelphia, and Charleston. The acts also legalized the hated Writs of Assistance. The American colonists were outraged.

Resisting the Townshend Acts

As soon as the Townshend Acts were passed, the colonists began to protest them. A well-to-do lawyer named John Dickinson wrote a series of essays called *Letters from a Farmer in Pennsylvania, to the Inhabitants of the British Colonies.* The essays captured the mood of the colonists, arguing that the Townshend duties were unethical. These essays were published in almost every colonial newspaper and reached a wide audience. Dickinson admitted that Parliament had the right to regulate colonial trade. However, he insisted, it was wrong to regulate trade with the purpose of raising revenue. Dickinson's argument was problematic and impractical, for it implied that the colonists should speculate upon the intent behind every trade law before accepting it.

In Massachusetts, patriots immediately resisted the Townshend Acts. The Massachusetts colonial assembly wrote a letter urging all the colonies to unite and create a petition of protest. They sent the letter to all the colonial legislatures. When England's secretary of state for America, Lord Hillsborough, heard about the letter circulating among the colonies, he ordered Francis Bernard, then the governor of Massachusetts, to recall the letter. He also ordered the other colonial assemblies not to discuss the letter. But his orders only made the colonists more defiant. The Massachusetts assembly met and by a vote of 92 to 17 decided not to recall the letter. Governor Bernard promptly dissolved the assembly. The same thing happened in other colonies when assemblies discussed the letter.

Rituals of Resistance

Throughout the colonies, protesters attached symbolic importance to the number ninety-two, because ninety-two assemblymen in Massachusetts had voted against recalling the protest letter. Ninety-two joined the number forty-five, which was already popular because of a well-known essay called "North Briton #45." Written by an Englishman named John Wilkes, the essay was sympathetic to the American cause. Wilkes was jailed after publishing his essay in England. Americans rallied around him. The Sons of Liberty made the number forty-five a symbol of resistance.

In Boston, silversmith Paul Revere cast a silver punch bowl that weighed forty-five ounces. The punch bowl was engraved with the names of the ninety-two legislators who had voted not to recall the Townshend Acts protest letter. The bowl commemorated their refusal to bow to pressure. Prominent Boston patriots, including John Adams and James Otis, drank forty-five toasts from the bowl. Similar public rituals involving the numbers forty-five and ninety-two occurred throughout the colonies.

In Charleston, South Carolina, protesters hung forty-five lanterns from a tree, then marched to a local tavern, carrying forty-five candles. In the tavern, they sat at forty-five tables set with forty-five bottles of wine, forty-five punch bowls, and ninety-two glasses. Public rituals of resistance helped educate ordinary people about the debate over British actions. Those who could not read the newspapers could witness these rituals and learn why so many people were frustrated with British policies.

Women also became involved in the resistance to the Townshend Acts. Although it was not considered polite or proper for them to be involved in politics, women established Daughters of Liberty chapters around the colonies. The Daughters of Liberty met in public. They would spin wool into yarn, encouraging all women to make homespun cloth rather than rely on imported English cloth. Their public displays of resistance inspired other women to do without imported goods. The Daughters of Liberty also boycotted tea. They drank coffee and made tea substitutes from local plants. Women of all classes, including the daughters of wealthy families, became involved in public spinning circles. In Boston, more than three hundred women swore in public that they would not drink any tea, except in cases of sickness (for tea was believed to have medicinal properties). In Wilmington, North Carolina, women burned their tea leaves.

Anger over the Townshend Acts caused people to picket stores whose owners imported British goods. In Boston, many merchants signed a one-year non-importation agreement. Merchants who refused to comply with the boycott were harassed by other merchants and by the public. Some imports were shipped back to England. John Hancock offered the use of his ship *Lydia* for free to those wishing to return British imports.

Nonimportation agreements like the one in Boston and public disdain for British goods caused the number of colonial imports from England to decrease sharply in 1769. Drops in sales caused factory owners in Manchester, England, to dismiss three out of every ten workmen.[1] Colonial importers were also adversely affected by the decline in British imports. Tradesmen, however, prospered. Colonists looked to them to make the goods they would not buy from England.

Protesting the Townshend Acts

The Sons of Liberty took to the streets once again, this time to protest the Townshend Acts. Marching to drums, they visited the homes of Boston's customs commissioners. On the anniversary of the Stamp Act's repeal, they hung effigies of the customs commissioners from the Liberty Tree. On February 22, 1770, they mobilized a crowd outside the home of North End merchant Theophilus Lillie because they believed he was breaking the nonimportation agreement. They erected a sign outside his shop, alerting people that Lillie was importing tea. Ebenezer Richardson, who had a reputation as a customs informer, lived next door to Lillie. He tried to take the sign down. The group outside Lillie's home grew angry. Some of the young boys in the crowd began throwing snowballs at Richardson, who went back into his house. The crowd began hurling stones and breaking his windows. Frightened, Richardson fired his gun at the crowd from an upstairs window. Christopher Seider, a twelve-year-old boy in the crowd, was mortally wounded by Richardson's fire.

Christopher Seider's funeral was attended by hundreds of Bostonians, including many schoolchildren. John Adams, the future president of the United States, recorded in his diary that he had never seen such a large funeral. The procession began at the Liberty Tree and continued along the main street, followed by hundreds of carriages.

Events in Massachusetts were beginning to worry Governor Bernard. He did not want to suffer the fate of Lieutenant Governor Thomas Hutchinson and have his house destroyed by an angry mob. He wanted British troops sent to Boston to protect royal officials and stop the mobs.

British Forces Are Sent to Boston

Earlier, in April 1768, the British naval commander at Halifax had sent H.M.S. *Romney*, a fifty-gun sloop of war in response to Bernard's request. A month after the *Romney*'s arrival, one of John Hancock's ships, the *Liberty*, was seized for smuggling Madeira wine. As customs officials were placing the sign of the Crown on the ship and preparing to tow it, waterfront workers were just leaving work. Many people recognized the *Romney*, which sometimes sent its longboats along the Boston waterfront to kidnap men to serve on its crew. This kind of kidnapping, known as impressment, was considered barbaric and illegal by colonists.

Quickly, a crowd of waterfront workers gathered and began hurling stones at the *Romney*'s crew. Then, they attacked the customs inspector and broke windows in the homes of several customs officers who lived nearby. At the home of customs collector Joseph Harrison, the mob seized a sailboat he was building, dragged it to Boston Common, and set it on fire.

The next day, customs officials and their families took refuge on the *Romney*, which transported them to Fort William for safety. The customs commissioners appealed for troops to be sent to Boston to curb mob violence.

In September 1768, two regiments from Halifax were sent to Boston. Governor Bernard had no place to house them, and naturally he got no help from the members of the Boston city council. The soldiers pitched their tents on the common, and some were housed in Faneuil Hall, as well as in the State House.

Colonists objected to the soldiers' presence and to their use of public property. Unwelcome and underpaid, many soldiers deserted the British Army. Seventy disappeared during the troops' first two weeks in Boston. To halt the desertion, British General Thomas Gage marched a soldier who had tried to desert in front of the regiments and had a firing squad execute him.

Local residents did not mix well with the soldiers. Bostonians saw the soldiers as a constant reminder of British oppression. The Redcoats (as British soldiers were called because of their red uniforms) paraded on Boston Common. They also patrolled the city day and night, sometimes harassing citizens and making lewd remarks to young women. At Boston Neck, the old entrance to the city, soldiers inspected travelers and their possessions. Civilians heckled the soldiers behind their backs, calling them "lobsterbacks" because of their red coats.

To supplement their pay, British troops took unskilled jobs in their off-duty hours, often for low wages. Local workers complained that they were taking jobs away from them. Soldiers were forbidden to shoot without orders, but fistfights frequently broke out between soldiers and workingmen.

On March 2, 1770, just a few days after the funeral of Christopher Seider, a soldier looking for part-time work came to a ship rigging factory (called a ropewalk) on Pearl Street in Boston. One of the factory workers taunted him, telling him that if he wanted work he could go clean the outhouse. The soldier hollered back that the worker should clean it himself. The shouting turned into a fight. The Redcoat was beaten, but he returned later with other members from his regiment and the fight turned into a large brawl. The ropewalk workers beat the Redcoats. The next day, another fight broke out, with the workers winning again. Two days later, with tensions running high, more violence between soldiers and civilians occurred.

The Boston Massacre

On the evening of Monday, March 5, 1770, passersby began throwing snowballs at soldiers standing guard near the State House. For reasons not fully understood, someone rang the church bells. When heard outside of normal church hours, the bells meant there was a fire or other cause to gather. Soon, people began to assemble outside the State House, wondering what the commotion was about. Some townspeople carried clubs. Others were worried that there was a fire, always a danger in cities with many wooden buildings so close together. Horse-drawn fire wagons arrived with buckets. Some people even shouted "Fire!"

The crowd began to taunt the Redcoats who were guarding the State House. The soldiers were not allowed to fire unless given orders by their captain. No order was given. Yet one of the soldiers fired into the crowd.

Eight others followed suit. Later, they would claim that they had heard the word "Fire!" They may well have thought their commander had given the order, for some people in the crowd had still been yelling "Fire" because of the ringing of the church bells. The Redcoats' commanding officer, Captain Thomas Preston, immediately ordered his men to cease firing. Five colonists had been fatally hit.

After the shootings, bells rang out again and even more citizens came into the streets. Drums summoned the colonial militia. Fearing retaliation, Captain Preston called out the entire British garrison. Though the crowd was ordered to disperse, the townspeople refused to leave the scene until the British soldiers were returned to their barracks. Captain Preston and the nine Redcoats who had fired at the crowd were placed in jail to await trial.

Crispus Attucks, a Massachusetts resident who was identified as black, but who may actually have been American Indian or biracial, was among the five victims. James Caldwell, a sailor, was also killed. Seventeen-year-old Samuel Maverick was hit by a ricocheting bullet as he ran. All three died immediately. Ropemaker Samuel Gray died within days from wounds sustained when the Redcoats fired upon the crowd. Patrick Carr, an Irish leather worker, succumbed to his wounds just days after the funeral for the other victims.

The funeral for the first four victims of the Boston Massacre was even more elaborate than the one for Christopher Seider. More than ten thousand people followed the coffins on their procession through Boston to the Old Granary Burial Ground, where the victims were laid to rest.

The trial of the British soldiers involved in the Boston Massacre was postponed for eight months. The colonists held so much hostility toward the men that Thomas Hutchinson, recently promoted from lieutenant governor to governor of Massachusetts, feared an earlier trial might set off more violence. The accused were eventually defended by none other than John Adams and Josiah Quincy, Jr., two renowned patriots. Adams and Quincy, both of whom were Sons of Liberty, wanted to show that the patriots disapproved of mob riots like the Boston Massacre, preferring orderly and peaceful political demonstrations. To make their point, Adams and Quincy volunteered their services and made sure that the soldiers had a fair trial. The soldiers were tried by their peers, and no Bostonians were allowed on the jury. Captain Preston was acquitted, along with six of the soldiers. Two of the soldiers, both involved in the earlier fights at Gray's ropewalk, were found guilty of manslaughter, a lesser crime than murder. Their right thumbs were branded with a hot iron for punishment. The favorable outcome of the trial prevented England from cracking down further on the city of Boston.

Bostonians did not know that on the very same day the Boston Massacre occurred, Lord North, the new prime minister of Great Britain, had signed the repeal of the Townshend duties. North believed that placing duties on trade within the empire was bad economic policy. In April, the news reached Boston that England's new prime minister had convinced Parliament to repeal all of the Townshend duties except the tax on tea. Lord North excepted tea from his decision because it was imported from China, not from within the empire.

Upon hearing the news, many merchants began importing British goods again. Some colonists, however, believed nonimportation should continue until the tea tax was also repealed.

News of the Boston Massacre spread quickly through the colonies. The five victims were commemorated as martyrs to the cause of freedom. Paul Revere made an engraving of the event that stretched the truth somewhat. It showed a British officer ordering a line of soldiers to fire on a peaceful crowd. This engraving was published throughout the colonies, fueling the resentment people felt toward the British. It also increased the fear of enslavement felt among the colonists. The stationing of troops in Boston seemed to be part of a plan to create a military state capable of enslaving the colonists. Radicals such as Samuel Adams played on these fears to arouse support for their cause. Colonists increasingly began to seek freedom from parliamentary authority. Still, they never stopped thinking of themselves as British citizens. They wished for the right to govern themselves much as they had in the years before 1763, but they still considered themselves loyal subjects of the king.

The Burning of the *Gaspee*

In June 1772, more than two years after the Boston Massacre, the British customs sloop H.M.S. *Gaspee* was stationed around Newport, Rhode Island, in order to crack down on colonial smuggling. The *Gaspee* chased the *Hannah*, a Rhode Island boat, into Narragansett Bay, hoping to find smuggled goods aboard. But the *Hannah*'s captain evaded capture by sailing into the shallow water off Warwick, Rhode Island. The *Gaspee* ran aground when it followed the *Hannah* into the shallow water. The *Hannah* escaped to Providence, where news of the incident spread rapidly.

H.M.S. *Gaspee* had long been the scourge of Rhode Island shippers. Knowing that the boat would remain aground until the early hours of the morning when the tide came in, a group of Providence men plotted the destruction of the sloop. Around midnight that evening, eight boats, with their oars wrapped in cloth to muffle the sound of rowing, reached the stranded *Gaspee*. One of the Providence men, Joseph Bucklin, shot the *Gaspee*'s commanding officer and wounded him. Then the Providence raiders overpowered the *Gaspee's* crew, sent them ashore, and burned the ship with all its contents.

Local citizens were jubilant when they learned of the destruction of the *Gaspee*. They considered it a coup for America. However, a royal investigation soon followed. The destruction of the *Gaspee*, the king's property, was a direct affront to the Crown. King George III himself offered a reward of two thousand pounds for information leading to the arrest of the *Gaspee* raiders.

Although many people in Providence knew who the raiders were, no one revealed their names. Those involved in the burning were never caught. The *Gaspee* inquiry, however, helped to create a committee of correspondence in Rhode Island. Eager to inform all Rhode Island towns of the *Gaspee* incident, Providence citizens began writing to warn the other towns of the importance of secrecy in the *Gaspee* case. Committees of correspondence were eventually established in all the colonies as a means of publicizing events and keeping the rural areas informed and involved.

Committees of Correspondence

At a town meeting in November 1772, Boston voters created a committee of correspondence of their own. Samuel Adams, who had proposed such a committee the previous year, became its head. Then fifty-two years old, Adams had long envisioned a communications network between and within the separate colonies. He believed such a network could be a powerful tool. If all the towns knew what was happening, it would be possible to reach a consensus. Then some kind of collective action could be taken based on that agreement.

Before the creation of the committees of correspondence, the resistance movement was concentrated in the colonies' seacoast towns and major cities. But the Boston Committee of Correspondence sent a list of grievances and instances where the colonists' rights had been infringed to every Massachusetts town. Most of the towns agreed with Boston's list of grievances. They declared their support for the Boston patriots. Committees of correspondence were eventually established in every colony. Samuel Adams's plan had worked. Events brewing in Boston would soon involve the entire colony in the protest movement against the tax on tea.

BOYCOTTING TEA

By 1773 the only Townshend duty still in effect was the tax on tea. Following the repeal of the other Townshend duties in 1770, some Americans had resumed drinking tea. Others continued to boycott the drink. Some drank tea secretly, not wanting anyone to know they indulged. It was not easy for colonists to give up their tea. Imagine asking every American adult today to go without coffee, especially his or her morning cup. Yet many colonists refused to buy tea in order to express their grievances with England.

The Significance of Tea

In order to understand the uproar about tea, it is important to understand just how much Americans enjoyed drinking it. Tea was a staple of the colonial diet in America, much like coffee is today.

The ritual of tea drinking was also socially significant. People socialized over tea in colonial America.

Colonists prided themselves on owning tea-drinking equipment, such as matching teacups and teapots. Inventories of colonial households show that in the first decades of the eighteenth century, wealthy families began to acquire matching teapots and teacups. Poorer families soon imitated the rich, buying the best tea sets they could afford. The apparatuses of tea, from tea sets to the tea leaves themselves, became indicators of social status. Wealthy families had expensive porcelain tea sets and the finest bohea, a particularly prized and expensive type of Chinese tea. Less well-to-do households made do with earthenware teapots and cheaper tea.

Since American potters did not yet have the technology to produce ceramics capable of holding very hot liquids, colonists imported ceramics from Staffordshire, England. In the 1760s, English potters had discovered how to make ceramics that were thinner, whiter, and harder than older pottery. Known as creamware, it became the first mass-produced British pottery. It became widely available at a cheaper cost than previous ceramics. Suddenly, even poor families could afford to buy ceramics. More Americans than ever purchased tea sets.

Tea was not only an indicator of status, but also a favorite drink. Everyone seemed to want it. In 1766, residents of a Philadelphia poorhouse demanded fine bohea, causing a confrontation with city officials.[1] Tea was so popular that when citizens protested the

Townshend Acts, their opposition was almost solely focused on the tax on tea. They started finding ways to get tax-free tea, creating a vast tea-smuggling network.

Smugglers of Tea

All the imported tea drunk in the American colonies was grown in Canton, China. The British East India Company acquired tea in Canton and shipped it to America, where it was subject to an import duty. Dutch traders also bought tea in Canton, but they sold it to smugglers, colonial businessmen with boats who lived in port cities. Smugglers purchased Dutch tea in Holland, or from the Dutch island of St. Eustacia in the Caribbean. They brought the Dutch tea into the colonies and sold it for less than the price of British-imported tea. They were able to make a good profit doing this. According to British law, only England was allowed to trade with the colonies. So colonial smugglers were breaking the law.

During the years of salutary neglect, when the Navigation Acts went unenforced, the smuggling of tea became fairly common. By the 1750s, smuggling was widespread. Since smuggled Dutch tea came from the same place as British tea, there was no way to tell smuggled tea from imported tea. With false documents and certificates of import, smuggled tea could easily be disguised as imported British tea. Thus, smuggling was hard to prove and smugglers were difficult to catch.

Many people living in coastal communities participated in smuggling networks. Their defiance of British law represented some of the first questioning of British authority, sparking early revolutionary stirrings. Historians believe this happened first in the colonial port cities in part because smuggling and a lack of respect for British law were already common there. When patriotic citizens began campaigning against British tea, smugglers continued to profit by importing Dutch tea.

Nonimportation of Tea

In 1768, a group of Boston merchants agreed not to import any British goods for one year. Some well-known firms, however, such as Thomas & Elisha Hutchinson and Richard Clarke & Sons, refused to comply. Loyal to the Crown, they continued to sell British tea. Boston patriots campaigned against these and other firms that did not go along with the nonimportation pact. They urged citizens to boycott these merchants. They put the names of these merchants in the papers and ridiculed them for continuing to import tea. By 1769, the Clarkes wrote to their British supplier, saying, "A great number of Inhabitants of this and other towns have agreed to disuse the drinking of India teas from a resentment of the [Townshend] Act. From [this] circumstance, teas [have] become a very slow Sale."[2] The amount of British tea entering the colonies was seriously reduced by the nonimportation pact. Tea smugglers, however, continued to operate during the boycott.

Many towns drafted resolves (decrees) supporting nonimportation. But inland merchants were disappointed when some of their coastal counterparts continued to violate the nonimportation agreement. Some gave up and chose to import British goods rather than lose money. While some individual colonists supported nonimportation and chose not to buy British tea, others continued to drink imported tea throughout the nonimportation period. One colonist wrote to a friend in England in 1769, expressing doubt that Americans would ever be able to do without tea:

> As to our people's quitting the use of tea, it is really a Joke. It would be full as reasonable to imagine that they will cease to drink New England Rum or Cyder. The flourishes in newspapers are designed only as deceptives and therefore ought to be treated as such. The Inhabitants are very strongly possessed in favor of it, & not capable of being actuated by principles of modern Patriotism . . . I don't believe there are ten chests of tea less consumed in this province in a year than there were before the Act took place . . .[3]

Although smuggled Dutch tea was still widely available, the British tea boycott did gain support throughout the colonies. Whole towns signed pledges promising not to buy English tea. Some may have continued to drink duty-free Dutch tea, although there was considerable pressure to drink no tea at all. Those who refused to sign the pledge might find their names on lists hung on the town hall door for all to see. Ladies' groups pledged to abstain from tea and sometimes even burned tea in public displays of their patriotism. The Daughters of Liberty drank tea substitutes when they met to spin thread in public, helping to promote the boycott of British imports.

The boycotts succeeded in hurting English business. Boycotts in Philadelphia and New York City almost stopped English tea imports entirely. For example, the city of New York had imported more than 350,000 pounds of tea from England in 1768. By 1770, however, New York City was importing only 147 pounds of English tea.

Finding Substitutes for Tea

Colonists experimented with alternatives to tea. Coffee became more popular, as did herbal teas. Some Americans tried, unsuccessfully, to grow the Chinese tea bush. The climate of the eastern seaboard did not oblige. Women brewed tea from a variety of local herbs and flowers. One of the most common substitutes for imported tea was made from the redroot bush, which grew throughout the swampy areas of New England. Known as Hyperion (or Labrador) tea, the drink had long been consumed by American Indians and Canadians and had a very strong flavor. Patriots sang the praises of Hyperion tea. They considered it the answer for those who were reluctant to give up imported tea. Boston printers Edes & Gill, renowned patriots, sold Hyperion tea in their office. Information on how to cure the leaves of the redroot bush and brew Hyperion tea was widely distributed. Boston newspapers promoted Hyperion, featuring jingles to encourage readers to try it.

To further persuade colonists to give up imported tea, patriots denounced bohea as an unhealthy and poisonous drink. They claimed it caused nervousness and a host of other ailments. Hyperion tea, they assured, caused none of these problems. Dr. Thomas Young, the first president of the North End Caucus, was one of the original members of the Boston Committee of Correspondence. He gave up tea for both political and medical reasons. Young wrote: "Tea is really a slow poison, and has a corrosive effect upon those who handle it. I have left it off since it became a political poison, and have since gained in firmness of constitution. My substitute is chamomile flowers."[4]

The Tea Act of 1773

With the Townshend duty on tea still in effect, Parliament passed the Tea Act in May 1773. Its purpose was to increase the revenue of the struggling British East India Company, which had been hurt by the colonial boycotts of British goods. The Tea Act allowed some of the duties paid on tea to be funneled back into the East India Company. It also stated that from then on, tea could be sold only by authorized merchants, called consignees. These consignees would be chosen by the East India

Company. This would give the company a monopoly on the tea trade, eliminating colonial middlemen and smugglers. Since the only people allowed to sell tea would be selected by the company, they could be sure no one would undersell them.

The net result of the Tea Act was cheaper tea for American consumers. Despite this benefit, Americans reacted negatively to the act. Some were angry because the tea, though less expensive, was still being taxed under the Townshend law. Others believed that the Tea Act forced them to accept Parliament's right to tax the American colonies. They worried that the Tea Act was the first step toward the creation of an East India Company monopoly on all colonial trade. Smugglers and other businessmen were also afraid of losing their livelihoods.

Colonists Resist the Tea Act

Across the colonies, news of the Tea Act caused Americans to mobilize. Patriots did not want to accept any tea subject to the tax. They hoped to persuade any newly arrived tea ships to return without unloading their cargoes in the colonies. To accomplish this, patriots encouraged the tea consignees to resign from their posts. A letter from a group calling themselves "The Mohawks" threatened the New York tea consignees. It said that anyone who helped unload or store the tea would receive an "unwelcome visit" from them.[5] Public pressure eventually caused all the New York consignees to resign. Similarly, patriots in Philadelphia held a mass meeting to discuss the Tea Act. Their outrage caused the Philadelphia consignees of tea to resign.

In Boston, Governor Hutchinson wanted to help the consignees of tea perform their duty, despite public opposition. Two of Hutchinson's own sons were tea consignees. In addition, British soldiers were already present in Boston—which had a history of rebellion—and they could deter mob violence if necessary.

The towns surrounding Boston pledged their support to the cause. They agreed that tea shipments should be resisted and, if necessary, returned. Samuel Adams asked the committees of correspondence in the neighboring towns of Brookline, Cambridge, Dorchester, and Roxbury to assemble at Faneuil Hall. There, the committees wrote to other Massachusetts towns. They declared that the only choice was to surrender like slaves and accept the tea or resist like free people. This communication among the different towns again caused Governor Hutchinson to worry. In November 1773, he wrote: "The infection [the growing rebellion] is industriously spreading, and the neighboring towns not only join their committees with the committee of Boston, but are assembled in town meetings to approve of the doings of the town of Boston."[6]

On November 17, 1773, a mob attacked the Clarke residence in the North End, throwing stones and breaking windows. The mob wanted merchant Richard

Clarke to resign his post as a consignee of tea. Clarke refused, but he and the other consignees feared for their safety. They asked the governor and the city council for protection. The consignees wanted to turn over their duty in landing and storing the tea to the government. The council, however, favored the patriot cause. It also knew Governor Hutchinson would be reluctant to act without its support. Therefore, it postponed its meeting and made no decision for the consignees. By stalling, the city council helped the patriot cause.

NIGHT OF THE MOHAWKS

On the evening of December 16, 1773, tensions were running at an all-time high in Boston. The seizure deadline for the *Dartmouth*'s cargo had arrived. Thousands of people had come into Boston from the countryside to seek a solution to the crisis. Faced with no way to return the tea cargoes, the people created a solution that would prevent them from having to accept the tea. The mass meeting at Old South Meeting House ended with the cries "Boston Harbor a tea-pot tonight!" and "The Mohawks are come!"

People pushed their way out of the meetinghouse and into the streets. Men crudely disguised as American Indians headed toward Griffin's Wharf, where the *Dartmouth*, the *Eleanor*, and the *Beaver* were docked. An estimated sixty men, both young and old, had already assembled at the wharf, beneath the light of the moon. They were wearing blankets and feathers and

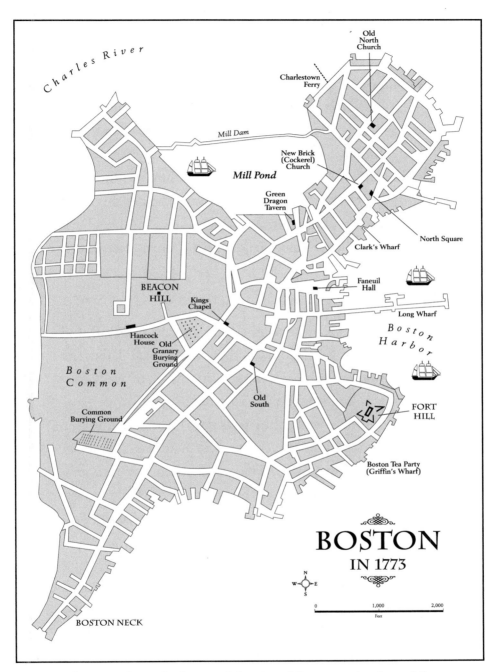

This map shows the layout of the city of Boston at the time of the Boston Tea Party.

had their faces darkly painted. Some of the men carried tomahawks.

These "Indians" called themselves Mohawks. They recognized one another by voice. They spoke in a garbled "Indian" jargon, which all of them seemed to understand. They acted quickly, boarding the three tea ships. On board each of the ships was a leader directing the Mohawks' activities. As men lined up on the wharf, the three leaders told them which ship to board and what to do.

Destroying the Tea

The Mohawks ordered the customs officials off the ships. The officials did as they were told. Then the Mohawks broke into groups. Some of them went into the ships' holds to attach rigging to the wooden tea chests. Others hoisted the chests onto the decks. Another group hacked into the chests with hatchets and shoveled the tea overboard. The smashed chests were also dumped overboard. Since the tide was low, the tea soon began to pile up, floating on the water. Some of the participants swept the piled-up tea away from the shore.

By the time the crowd from Old South Meeting House—between one thousand and two thousand people—had made its way down Milk Street and onto Hutchinson Street and Griffin's Wharf, the steady cracks of the Mohawks' hatchets could be heard from blocks away. The crowd grew silent as it witnessed the destruction. The three tea ships held approximately one hundred thousand pounds of tea. The value of the tea was about ten thousand British pounds. Within four hours, the Mohawks had emptied all 342 chests of tea into the sea.

Though the tea was within their grasp, the crowd, except for one man, did not try to take the tea that washed toward them. An Irish immigrant known as Captain Conner attempted to fill the lining of his coat with tea and was attacked by the crowd of spectators. They tore off his coat and beat him.

Royal authorities made no attempt to break up the tea party. Admiral John Montagu, head of the British Navy in Boston, witnessed the destruction from a house near Griffin's Wharf. Later, he claimed that he could not have broken up the vandals without firing into the crowd, risking the lives of many bystanders. The patriots' decision to move the ships from Fort William to Griffin's Wharf had paid off. It saved them from the cannon.

The entry in the *Dartmouth*'s logbook for the night of Thursday, December 16, read:

> Between six and seven o'clock this evening, came down to the wharf a body of about one thousand people, among them were a number dressed and whooping like Indians. They came on board the ship, and after warning myself and the custom-house officers to get out of the way, they undid the hatches and went down the hold, where was eighty whole and thirty-four half chests of tea, which they hoisted upon deck and cut the chests to pieces and hove the tea all overboard, where it was damaged and lost.[1]

By 9:00 P.M., the last tea chest had been dumped. Some of the Mohawks removed their shoes and dumped out any tea leaves that were stuck in them. Forming a line, the Mohawks then marched toward town to the tune of a fife. Admiral Montagu, watching from an overhanging window, shouted to the Mohawks as they left Griffin's Wharf, "Well, boys, you've had a fine, pleasant evening for your Indian caper, haven't you? But mind, you've got to pay the fiddler yet!"

Lendall Pitts, one of the Mohawks' leaders, shouted back, taunting the admiral: "Oh, never mind! Never mind, squire! Just come out here, if you please, and we'll settle the bill in two minutes."[2]

Who Were the Mohawks?

While Samuel Savage and Samuel Adams were leading the meeting at Old South on the night of December 16, many of the tea party participants were already dressed. They were just waiting for the signal to act.

There were probably between 110 and 130 men who participated in the tea party. The Mohawks came from all parts of Boston and the surrounding area. One group of seventeen men from Lebanon, Maine, came down to Boston expressly to help destroy the tea. They put on their disguises at a tavern near Griffin's Wharf. A doctor, merchants, teachers, and farmers all participated in the tea party. But the majority of the "Mohawks" were artisans—carpenters, masons, blacksmiths, and young apprentices. Paul Revere, a silversmith and renowned patriot, was among them. Most of the men became involved in the tea party through their membership in groups such as the Freemasons, the Sons of Liberty, and the North End Caucus. A good number of the participants must have been Freemasons, for the lodge record book for the night of December 16, 1773, said: "The lodge met and closed on account of the few members in attendance. Adjourned until tomorrow evening."[3]

It was nearly 10:00 P.M. when the Mohawks finally returned to their homes and taverns. Despite advance preparations, the tea party had been planned in such secrecy that many women were shocked when their husbands came home that night in costumes. One participant, Joseph Palmer, came to his door with two friends. His wife screamed at the sight of the three "Indians." "Don't be frightened, Betty," Palmer said to his wife. "It is I. We have only been making a little salt-water tea."[4] Many Mohawks found tea leaves that had fallen into their boots or gotten stuck inside their clothes. Some bottled the leaves so that they could tell their grandchildren about the tea party. Others immediately burned the leaves.

Not all of the participants had been involved in the tea party's planning. Many joined in on the spur of the moment. Samuel Sprague, a twenty-year-old apprentice stonemason, was on his way to visit the woman he was courting when he ran into a group of friends. They informed him that there was a commotion at Griffin's

Wharf. Heading there with his friends, Sprague saw the Mohawks destroying the tea chests and longed to join them. He looked around for some means of disguising himself. Climbing onto the low roof of a nearby building, he smeared his face with soot from its chimney. After joining the Mohawks, Sprague recognized his master, the man to whom he was apprenticed, as one of the "Indians." The two worked side by side. Afterward, Sprague recalled, the two never spoke of their involvement in the tea party. All of those who joined in the tea party kept their participation a secret, and the event remained shrouded in mystery for years.

Some of the young apprentices who took part lived with Tory masters. They had to sneak out of their masters' homes to join the mayhem at the wharf. Benjamin Simpson, a nineteen-year-old apprentice bricklayer, was undisguised when he joined the Mohawks. He helped shovel tea off the deck of one of the boats. Since the tide was low, the dumped tea began to pile up and float upon the water. It grew so high that it fell back on board some of the ships. Many of the young men who joined the action after it started helped to shovel the tea back overboard and sweep the decks. They also helped the Mohawks raise the derricks (the hoisting apparatuses) on the boats and lift the heavy tea chests out of the cargo holds.

Robert Sessions was a young man working for a lumber merchant in Boston. His employer came home from the meeting at Old South, announcing that tea was being dumped in the harbor. Sessions immediately asked for permission to go down to the wharf. Seeing that the Mohawks needed help, Sessions boarded one of the ships, undisguised, and began sweeping tea. Afterward, Sessions was afraid of being arrested. He feared that he might have been recognized. He left Boston and returned to his parents' home in Connecticut.

William Tudor was a law student in the office of John Adams. He was headed to Griffin's Wharf that night with a number of men who had gathered together and disguised themselves at Fort Hill. On the way, Tudor saw a British officer. The officer drew his sword on the band of Mohawks. According to Tudor, one of the Mohawks then brandished a pistol. The Mohawk told the officer, "The path is wide enough for us all; we have nothing to do with you, and intend you no harm; if you keep your own way peaceably, we shall keep ours."[5]

David Kinnison lived longer than any of the other participants in the tea party. He died in 1852 at the age of 115. Kinnison was among the seventeen men who had come down from Maine specifically to take part in the tea party. Ready for a confrontation, they were armed with muskets, bayonets, tomahawks, and clubs. The Mainers had made a pact. They would stand by one another to the end, revealing no names. Throughout his long life, whenever he was asked about the tea party,

Kinnison explained that those who participated had all pledged never to reveal one another's names.

Joshua Wyeth, a journeyman blacksmith, was only sixteen when he helped the Mohawks dump the tea. He recalled the mood of the men that night:

> We were merry, in an undertone, at the idea of making so large a cup of tea for the fishes, but were as still as the nature of the case would admit, using no more words than were absolutely necessary. We stirred briskly in the business from the moment we left our dressing room. I never worked harder in my life.[6]

Lifting the heavy tea chests was a difficult job. Twenty-three-year-old Samuel Hobbs, a tanner from Roxbury, estimated that the weight of one chest of bohea was about 360 pounds. Besides the heavy lifting, the men also had to take great care not to disturb the ships' other cargoes or to harm the ships themselves or their rigging. Other than the tea floating in the harbor, the only item damaged aboard the ships that night was a padlock. The next day, one of the patriots replaced it with a new lock.

Mohawk Disguises

The best-disguised Mohawks were those of prominent families and position in Boston, such as Paul Revere and Dr. Thomas Young. Some of the young men who joined in the action that night had worn no disguises at all. Many participants disguised themselves by daubing their faces with paint, soot, lampblack, or grease. Others darkened their faces with charcoal and burned cork in an attempt to conceal their identities. Dressed in ragged clothes, old frocks, red woolen sleeping gowns, or old blankets, they were a strange-looking crew. Some donned Indian costumes and actual Indian clothing and headdresses.

Benjamin Russell, a schoolboy at the time, saw his father and a neighbor, Thomas Moore, smearing each other's faces with lampblack and red ocher on the night of the tea party. Peter Slater, a fourteen-year-old rope-maker's apprentice, overheard the excitement and jumped out his bedroom window. He went to a nearby blacksmith's shop, where a disguised man told him to put charcoal on his face, tie a handkerchief around his shirt, and follow him.

Peter Edes, the son of printer Benjamin Edes, recalled how a number of men met at the Edes home to don their disguises. Peter was a teenager, and he was not allowed to enter the room where the men gathered. The men did not want to be seen by anyone else. "I recollect perfectly well that on the day [afternoon] preceding the evening on which the tea was destroyed, the Indians met at my father's house," wrote Peter Edes. "I was busily employed in squeezing lemons and making punch for them. They there disguised themselves in the garb of Indians and went from thence in the evening to the wharf where the ships lay."[7]

The tea party participants dressed as Indians for several reasons. First, they wanted to disguise themselves. No one wanted to be caught destroying private property. The punishment in this case was likely to be severe. Second, the American Indian had long been a symbol of liberty for the colonists. Paul Revere used Indians in his engravings to symbolize the new American nation. He even designed the Massachusetts state seal with an Indian figure. Earlier in 1773, when New York patriots told the consignees of tea to resign, they signed their warning, "The Mohawks." This may have prompted the Boston Tea Party organizers to call themselves Mohawk Indians.

Who Planned the Tea Party?

The Boston Tea Party had been organized in advance. Just who planned it, however, is still a mystery. Like the identity of many of the perpetrators, the planning of the tea party has remained a secret throughout history. Most likely, the Sons of Liberty and other patriot organizations planned the tea party before the night of December 16. They needed to gather the Mohawks and prepare them. Somehow, the Mohawks knew where to meet and how to disguise themselves. Many details about the night of December 16, 1773, are still unknown. However, most historians believe Samuel Adams and other key leaders of the Massachusetts patriot movement were involved in planning the tea party.

The patriots believed that destroying the tea was the only way to end the stalemate, which they feared might otherwise end with the eventual unloading of the tea. They had already decided not to pay any tax that was levied for the sole purpose of raising revenue from the colonies. The other colonies had sent letters chastising Boston for having previously imported dutied tea. One letter from Philadelphia, published in Boston on December 13, read: "You [Boston] have failed us . . . and we fear you will suffer this [tea] to be landed."[8] Spurred on by these letters, the patriots were determined to take action.

The tea party was probably planned during the December 13 mass meeting of citizens from Boston and the neighboring towns. It was not a spontaneous act, and it required careful planning. It was a very serious undertaking. The destruction of so much cargo could be a capital crime for those caught. The perpetrators could be jailed or even executed. Therefore, the planners wanted to make sure they had done all they could before resorting to this act. Samuel Adams made this clear in his final remark at the December 16 meeting at the Old South Meeting House. He announced that they had tried everything in their power to have the ships sent back. There was nothing more, he said, that those at the meeting could do. This was his justification for what was to come, and it was the Mohawks' cue to act.

On December 17, 1773, John Adams wrote in his diary: "This destruction of the tea is so bold, so daring, so firm, intrepid, and inflexible, and it must have so important consequences and so lasting, that I cannot but consider it as an epocha [sic] in history . . ."[9] Adams's assessment was astute: The tea party would prove to be an event with far-reaching consequences for Boston and all of colonial America. As Admiral Montagu had reminded the Mohawks as they left Griffin's Wharf, the colonists would have to pay for their actions.

Chapter 6

THE TRIGGER OF REVOLUTION

By the morning after the tea party, a full account of the event had been prepared by the Boston Committee of Correspondence to be given to other towns and colonies. Paul Revere, himself believed to have been a participant, was asked to deliver the letter to New York. He rode there on horseback, and his news was received with great excitement. The news then traveled to Philadelphia via another courier. The letter Revere carried said, in part:

> Gentlemen—we inform you in great haste that every chest of tea on board the three ships in this town was destroyed this last evening without the least injury to the vessels or any other property. Our enemies must acknowledge that these people have acted upon pure and upright principle.[1]

Crowds cheered upon receiving the news in New York, and bells were rung in the city of Philadelphia. The Carolinas also signaled their approval by sending letters of praise to Boston. But despite the colonists' joyful reactions, the Mohawks did not brag about their deeds. No one wanted to be discovered and charged with the crime. One participant, sixteen-year-old Joshua Wyeth, remembered, "We pretended to be as zealous to find out the perpetrators as the rest, and were all so close and loyal, that the whole affair remained in Egyptian darkness."[2] All of the participants recognized the need for secrecy. Only one man, a barber named Eckley, was arrested in connection with the tea party. He was eventually let go for lack of evidence. But the Sons of Liberty provided for his family while he was in prison, and they helped secure his release, most likely by paying to get him out of jail. The informer who turned in Eckley was later tarred and feathered and carted through the streets by supporters of the patriot movement.

News of the tea party reached England by boat, and then a reply from the Crown returned by boat. As a result, Boston did not receive word from England about the tea party until nearly five months after the incident occurred. In the meantime, the Boston consignees of tea took refuge in Fort William. Posters calling for their tarring and feathering had appeared around the city. Not wanting to risk being subjected to this torture, the tea consignees chose to go into hiding.

Aftermath of the Tea Party

The Boston Tea Party had ripple effects throughout the colonies. Elsewhere, shipments of tea were seized and destroyed, sometimes by people in Indian costume. A traveling salesman was accosted in Shrewsbury, Massachusetts, and forced to throw his tea into a bonfire built by locals. In Lyme, Connecticut, another peddler was forced to burn his one hundred pounds of tea. A Weston, Massachusetts, innkeeper was accused of selling imported tea. A group of Weston residents, dressed as Indians, attacked his inn.

A few days after the tea party, John Adams wrote to a friend, James Warren, in Rhode Island, where a tea ship was reportedly headed. Adams wondered whether any "Vineyard, Mashpee, or Metapoisett Indians" might attack the ship.[3]

The passengers on the first ship to reach London from Boston after the tea party were summoned by British authorities. Whether traveling for business or pleasure or simply returning home, the men aboard were called before the Privy Council and questioned about the tea party. The council hoped to learn the names of some of the perpetrators in order to punish them. The tea party had been carried out with such secrecy, however, that the passengers truthfully did not have any information to supply. When the passengers were unable to name any of the participants, British officials grew annoyed. The king wanted to try the perpetrators on treason charges. Unable to learn any names, British officials considered forms of punishment for the whole colony. Benjamin Franklin, who was working as a colonial agent in London, warned Bostonians that Parliament was considering drastic punishment.

Parliament Punishes Boston

In May 1774, Boston learned of its punishment. News of the newly enacted Boston Port Act arrived. To make the Bostonians pay for destroying the tea, Parliament had voted to close Boston Harbor, effective June 1, 1774, to both incoming and outgoing ships until all the destroyed tea was paid for. Only coastal trade in food and firewood would be permitted. The Boston Port Act officially sealed off Boston's waterways.

Shipping was essential to the economy of Boston, a coastal city. Many people's jobs were connected closely with the harbor. Thousands of Bostonians lost their jobs when the harbor was closed. Some people in England had opposed the closing of Boston Harbor. Benjamin Franklin had strongly objected. He told Parliament that the closing of the harbor would only make it harder for Bostonians to pay for the damaged tea. But Franklin's warning was ignored. England was determined to punish Boston for the tea party.

Bostonians reacted to the bad news by protesting the Boston Port Act at a town meeting held in Faneuil Hall. They voted not to pay for the tea that had been destroyed. They urged the other colonies to join them in a boycott of all English goods. To this end, the committee of correspondence was put into action. Samuel Adams felt that it was time for the colonies to unite. If England could do this to Boston, what would prevent it from doing the same to the other colonies as well? Bostonians wrote to other towns and colonies, asking for their support. The letters expressed the belief that surely Boston would "not be left to struggle alone" in this crisis.[4] Paul Revere rode to New York with the news of the Boston Port Act.

Letters of support flowed into Boston from around the colonies. Many towns promised to boycott British goods. Some of them publicly burned copies of the Boston Port Act. Even towns that had disapproved of the tea party now showed their support. One resident of Middletown, Connecticut, wrote, "Even the old farmers who were So Sorry that So much Tea should be wasted . . . Now Say that they will Stand by the Bostonians and do everything in their power to Assist them."[5]

Hearing of the closing of Boston's port, South Carolina sent shipments of rice to help feed people who had lost their jobs. The South Carolinians raised the money by staging a play. People who wanted to see the play were asked to donate rice as the price of admission. The rice, like other donations, was shipped to the nearest open port and then brought to Boston in wagons. Tiny towns in Connecticut donated hundreds of sheep for the relief of Boston. Israel Putnam, a farmer from Pomfret, Connecticut, who would later serve as a general in the Revolutionary War, led 130 sheep from his farm all the way to Boston. More than a thousand bushels of grain arrived from Quebec. Other colonies donated food, firewood, and clothing. Individuals helped by donating a calf, a cord of wood, or a pound of cornmeal.

The Intolerable Acts

The closing of Boston Harbor was the first of four measures Parliament enacted against the colonies after the Boston Tea Party. Officially known to the British as the Coercive Acts, these measures, despised by the colonists, came to be called the Intolerable Acts by Americans. The acts were designed to prevent future uprisings.

Some of the Intolerable Acts affected the colony of Massachusetts alone, but other provisions were aimed at the colonies as a whole. The Massachusetts Government Act changed the colony's charter. Parliament substituted an appointed council for Massachusetts' elected council so that lawmakers could be chosen by British officials. Next, Parliament outlawed special town meetings, such as the mass meetings that had taken place before the tea party. They did not want the people to be able to plan any more insurrections. Then, it increased the powers of the governor. The Justice Act affected all of the colonies, stating that anyone who murdered a person while trying to stop a riot could be tried outside the colony where the murder occurred. This was an attempt to prevent sympathetic local juries. Finally, Parliament passed the Quartering Act, which allowed military leaders to house their troops wherever they saw fit in any colony. They could even force citizens to house troops in their homes.

The Intolerable Acts devastated the citizens of Massachusetts and were received poorly in the other colonies as well. It seemed as if England were trying to enslave the colonies after all.

The Quebec Act

The final blow came when Parliament passed the Quebec Act in the summer of 1774. Ever since England had conquered the former French colony in Canada, tensions had run high between Catholics and Protestants living in Quebec. The Quebec Act was intended to ease these problems. It granted greater religious freedom to the Catholics living in Canada.

Although the Quebec Act was not intended to punish the colonists, the Americans considered it another intolerable act. The majority of American colonists were Protestants. They viewed Catholics with suspicion. They did not want Catholicism to be encouraged in the Americas. Protestant colonists feared that by encouraging Catholicism, Parliament was encouraging the oppression of Protestants.

The colonists also hated the Quebec Act because it granted the region east of the Mississippi and north of the Ohio River to Quebec. This land had already been claimed by some of the American colonies. The colonists believed the Quebec Act was another attempt by Parliament to punish them.

The Colonists Suffer

The Intolerable Acts and the Quebec Act oppressed all of the colonists. With the closure of their port, Bostonians were hit especially hard. They lived like an enslaved populace. The city of Boston had become a police state. More troops were brought to the city, and British warships blocked the harbor. Frustrated, Governor Hutchinson resigned his post and moved to England. General Thomas Gage was sent to Boston to become the next royal governor. The seat of the Massachusetts colony's government was moved out of Boston to Salem. The colony's custom house was moved to Plymouth. Boston was no longer the hub of the colony.

Samuel Adams and the other patriot leaders did not believe Bostonians had committed any crime during the tea party. They were against paying for the destroyed tea. They argued that it had been criminal for the East India Company to send the tea against their wishes. Since the Intolerable Acts punished all

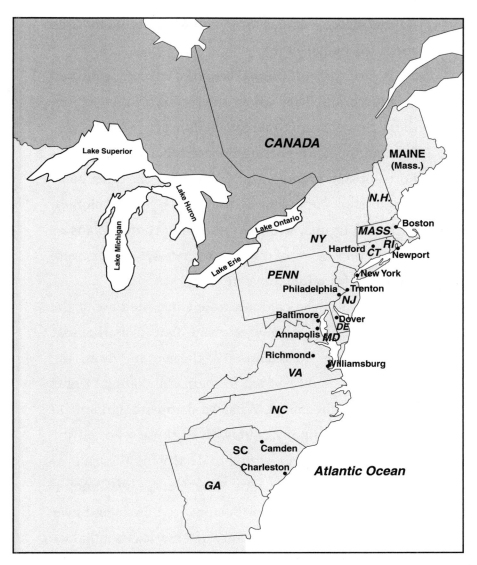

The Thirteen Colonies in 1773. *The Boston Tea Party and the closing of Boston's port helped inspire the leaders of the thirteen original colonies to unite in their opposition to British rule.*

the colonies for the tea party, the Boston patriots wanted all the colonies to vote on what should be done about the damaged tea.

Boston patriots wanted to start a boycott against all British goods. They asked their countrymen to join them. Some Boston merchants, however, simply relocated and began importing through other Massachusetts ports. Boston patriots tried to convince the other colonies to stop importing British goods. Some colonies, such as Virginia, drew up non-importation plans as soon as they heard of the Boston Port Act. Others were not ready for a total boycott.

Still, all of the colonies were concerned about the Intolerable Acts. They worried that if Parliament could change Massachusetts' charter at whim, the same thing could happen to them. All colonial rights were being threatened. What was happening in Boston could happen in any colony. Even those who felt the Bostonians had been wrong in destroying the tea now took pity on them. In June 1774, George Washington remarked, "The cause of Boston . . . now is and ever will be considered as the cause of America (not that we approve their conduct in destroying the tea)."[6] That June, the colonies decided to call an intercolonial congress in Philadelphia. They wanted to discuss what to do about the Intolerable Acts.

The First Continental Congress

Fifty-five of the colonies' leading political figures were nominated as delegates to the First Continental Congress. Only Georgia did not send delegates to Philadelphia in September 1774. With a population of only thirty-three thousand people, half of them black slaves, and a frontier threatened by angry American Indians, Georgia relied on support from England. In fact, Parliament gave more to Georgia's budget than did all of Georgia's taxpayers combined. As a result, Georgia did not dare offend the mother country and refused to send delegates.

The other colonies, however, were eager to participate. Samuel Adams, his cousin John Adams, Robert Treat Paine, and Thomas Cushing were chosen to represent Massachusetts. The delegates were given a great send-off as they started on their trip to Philadelphia in August.

The delegates met to discuss how the colonies should respond to the Intolerable Acts. Most patriots still hoped to make peace with England. Only the most radical among them were ready for independence. Still, the delegates voted to back Boston's resistance to the Intolerable Acts. The congress also endorsed a set of resolutions offered by the Massachusetts delegation. Called the Suffolk Resolves, these resolutions stated that the Intolerable Acts were unconstitutional because England could not revoke the rights granted in the charter of the Massachusetts colony. They also called for the military training of the colonists so that they could defend themselves if necessary. Finally, the resolves requested that all Massachusetts counties immediately boycott British goods.

The First Continental Congress endorsed a boycott of British goods by all the colonies, to begin after December 1, 1774. It decided to give England until September 1775 to address colonial grievances. If the colonies' concerns were not met by that time, the colonists would take further action. American exports to England and its other colonies would cease. The Americans were planning commercial warfare.

The First Continental Congress also endorsed a document called the Declaration of Colonial Rights and Grievances, whose final version was drafted by John Adams. The declaration listed the rights to which the colonists felt they were entitled, such as the right to consent to only legislation that was beneficial to the colonies. It also stated their refusal to accept taxation on internal commerce, such as the Townshend duties had required. Finally, the document called for the repeal of the Intolerable Acts and the Quebec Act, which the American colonists considered unconstitutional.

In addition to making the declaration, the delegates composed letters to England demanding the return of the freedom they had enjoyed up until the year 1763. Before adjourning, the Continental Congress agreed to meet again in May 1775, unless the grievances were resolved before that time. The congress had been in session for a month. In October 1774, the delegates returned to their home colonies.

The American colonies were now united in their opposition to the Intolerable Acts. They were also determined to impose economic sanctions against England. They had decided that Parliament had no right to legislate for them without direct representation. They were prepared to defend their beliefs with military force. Although few realized it then, the colonists were on the road to revolution. The Boston Tea Party had helped get them there.

The Trigger of Revolution

The Boston Tea Party caused England to punish the colonies with the Intolerable Acts. But the Intolerable Acts aroused the colonists to united action. They held a congress to determine their future. The colonists' opposition to the Intolerable Acts brought them closer together and set them on a course that would lead to war with England.

The Boston Tea Party was the event that sparked the agitation that grew into united opposition to England. Supporting Boston became a common cause for all of the colonies. Like Boston, the other colonies realized that their economic interests were different from England's. They did not want to serve simply as a means of revenue for the mother country. They wanted the freedom to govern themselves and to conduct business for their own benefit. The colonists had finally realized that their understanding of politics was different from that of their English cousins. Americans had their own ideas about government. And they were ready to defend their right to self-rule.

☆ TIMELINE ☆

1620—The Mayflower sails from Plymouth, England; The passengers start the Plymouth Colony.

1630—Massachusetts Bay Colony is founded.

1651—First Navigation Act is passed.

1691—Massachusetts Bay Colony absorbs the Plymouth Colony.

1754—France and England fight the Seven Years' War (called the French and Indian War in America) over control of North America.

1760—George III becomes king of England.

1763—End of the Seven Years' War; France cedes its North American territories to Great Britain; George Grenville becomes prime minister of England; British crackdown on smuggling.

1764—Parliament passes the Sugar Act and the Currency Act; James Otis publishes *The Rights of the British Colonies Asserted and Proved*.

1765—The Stamp Act is passed; Patrick Henry drafts the Virginia Stamp Act Resolves; The Sons of Liberty form to resist the Stamp Act; Stamp Act Congress meets in New York City; Stamp Act riots occur in Boston; A mob destroys Lieutenant Governor Thomas Hutchinson's home; Lord Rockingham replaces Grenville as prime minister; North End Caucus forms.

1766—Parliament repeals the Stamp Act but passes the Declaratory Act, stating its right to tax the colonies.

1767—The Townshend Acts are passed; John Dickinson publishes *Letters from a Farmer in Pennsylvania*.

1768—The Massachusetts Assembly refuses to recall its protest letter; Governor Bernard dissolves the assembly.

1769—Colonial imports from England sharply decrease due to nonimportation agreements.

1770—Lord North becomes prime minister; Townshend duties are repealed except the tax on tea; The Boston Massacre takes place; Five colonists are killed.

1772—Citizens of Providence, Rhode Island, burn the British sloop *Gaspee*; The committees of correspondence are formed around the colonies.

1773—*May*: Parliament passes the Tea Act.

November 28: The first ship subject to the new tea tax, the *Dartmouth*, arrives in Boston Harbor.

December 7: Two more tea ships, the *Beaver* and the *Eleanor*, arrive.

December 16: The Boston Tea Party takes place.

1774—Parliament passes the Intolerable Acts; Boston Port Act is passed; Boston Harbor is closed; Colonial towns and cities send supplies to relieve Boston; The Quebec Act grants religious freedom to Catholics in Canada; First Continental Congress convenes in Philadelphia; The colonists agree on a non-importation pact.

1775—Battles of Lexington and Concord begin the Revolutionary War.

☆ CHAPTER NOTES ☆

Chapter 1. Tension Builds in Boston

1. Francis Samuel Drake, *Tea Leaves* (Boston: A. O. Crane, 1884), p. xliii.

2. Letter from Dr. Cooper to Dr. Franklin, Massachusetts Historical Society (MHS) papers.

3. Benjamin Labaree, *The Boston Tea Party* (New York: Oxford University Press, 1964), p. 118.

4. "The Boston Tea Party," *The Boston Globe Special Supplement* (Boston: Globe Newspaper Co., 1974), p. 41.

5. Ibid.

6. Boston Gazette, December 13, 1773.

7. Drake, p. lxiii.

8. Ibid., p. lxiv.

9. Ibid.

10. Labaree, p. 141.

Chapter 2. We Want to Be Left Alone

1. "The Boston Tea Party," *The Boston Globe Special Supplement* (Boston: Globe Newspaper Co.,1974), p. 7.

2. *A People and a Nation* (Boston: Houghton Mifflin Co., 1990), vol. 1, p. 117.

3. "The Boston Tea Party," *Boston Globe*, p. 12.

4. *A People and a Nation*, vol. 1, p. 117.

5. "The Boston Tea Party," *Boston Globe*, p.13.

6. Francis Samuel Drake, *Tea Leaves* (Boston: A. O. Crane, 1884), pp. xxii–xxiv.

Chapter 3. The Colonists Resist

1. "The Boston Tea Party," *The Boston Globe Special Supplement*, (Boston: Globe Newspaper Co., 1974), p. 13.

Chapter 4. Boycotting Tea

1. T. H. Breen, "An Empire of Goods," *Colonial America: Essays in Politics and Social Development* (New York: McGraw-Hill, 1993), p. 387.

2. Benjamin Labaree, *The Boston Tea Party* (New York: Oxford University Press, 1964), p. 33.

3. Ibid., p. 31.

4. Francis Samuel Drake, *Tea Leaves* (Boston: A. O. Crane, 1884), p. clxxii.

5. Labaree, p. 95.

6. "The Boston Tea Party," *Boston Globe*, p. 37.

Chapter 5. Night of the Mohawks

1. Francis Samuel Drake, *Tea Leaves* (Boston: A. O. Crane, 1884), p. lxix.

2. "The Boston Tea Party," *The Boston Globe Special Supplement* (Boston: Globe Newspaper Co., 1974), p. 60.

3. Ibid., p. 51.

4. Wesley S. Griswold, *The Night the Revolution Began: The Boston Tea Party, 1773* (Brattleboro, Vt.: The Stephen Greene Press, 1972), p. 106.

5. Drake, p. lxxx.

6. "The Boston Tea Party," *Boston Globe*, p. 52.

7. Letter of Peter Edes to grandsons, February 16, 1836, Bangor, Maine, from Massachusetts Historical Society collections.

8. *Boston Gazette*, December 13, 1773.

9. Lyman Butterfield, ed., *Diary of John Adams* (Boston: Massachusetts Historical Society, 1961), vol. 2, pp. 85–86.

Chapter 6. The Trigger of Revolution

1. John Harris, ed., "The Boston Tea Party," *Boston Globe*, 1976, p. 61.

2. Ibid., p. 54.

3. Bruce E. Johansen, "Mohawks, Axes and Taxes, Images of the American Revolution," *History Today*, April 1985, vol. 35, p. 13.

4. Massachusetts Historical Society broadside, Boston, May 12, 1774, from the Boston Committee of Correspondence circular letter.

5. Benjamin Labaree, *The Boston Tea Party* (New York: Oxford University Press, 1964), pp. 220–221.

6. Ibid., p. 234.

☆ FURTHER READING ☆

Books

Crompton, Samuel Willard. *The Boston Tea Party: Colonists Protest the British Government.* New York: Chelsea House Publications, 2011.

Cunningham, Kevin. *The Boston Tea Party.* New York: Scholastic, 2012.

Freedman, Russell. *The Boston Tea Party.* New York: Holiday House, 2012.

Hakim, Joy. *A History of US: Making Thirteen Colonies: 1600–1740.* New York: Oxford University Press, 2007.

Krull, Kathleen. *What Was the Boston Tea Party?* New York: Grosset & Dunlap, 2013.

Stein, R. Conrad. *The Boston Tea Party.* Chicago, Ill.: Children's Press, 1998.

Trueit, Trudi Strain. *The Boston Tea Party.* Chicago, Ill.: Children's Press, 2008.

☆ INDEX ☆